BELIEVERS
ARE
RECEIVERS

BELIEVERS ARE RECEIVERS

BY
COLUMBUS O'BANNER JR.

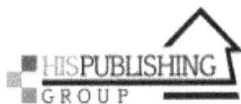

HISPUBLISHING GROUP

www.hispubg.com
A division of HISpecialists, llc

Inquiries should be addressed to
HIS Publishing Group, 1402 Corinth St., Suite 131
Dallas, Texas 75215.

Published by HIS Publishing Group
Division of Human Improvement Specialists, llc
Contact: info@hispubg.com

All Scripture quotations taken from the Kings James Bible

Cover logo designed by Margo Hemphill of
Oneway Promotional Products

Special Tribute to Columbus O'Banner Ministries
Publication Administrator Anita Berry

ISBN: 978-0-9836367-9-3

Printed and bound in the United States of America

ACKNOWLEDGEMENTS

I would like to acknowledge God my Father, Jesus my Savior and Lord, and the Holy Spirit who is my Teacher. Without The Lord speaking to my spirit, this book never would have been written, nor published. Without God my Father I would be a failure in life.

I give God all the glory for all the good things that have happened and will continue to happen in my life. I am very thankful for God my Father entrusting me with precious revelation in my spirit and allowing me to share it with other people in the earth.

DEDICATIONS

I would like to dedicate this book to my wife Barbara, who has been a blessing in my life. I thank The Lord, for her love, faithfulness, and support.

To our Children, Marquis L. O'Banner and his wife DeMarias, Alisha Chandler and her husband Mario, Joycelyn D. O'Banner, and Victoria H. O'Banner.

To our seven grandchildren Elijah, Elyse, Caleb, Daysean, Dajah, Kaiden, and Zhane'.

To my Father Columbus O'Banner Sr. who was promoted to Heaven at the age of 92 on September 23, 2013.

To my Mother Flora Mae O'Banner.

To all of my Father's and Mother's children, grandchildren and great grandchildren.

A special tribute to my sister Sharon Ann Alexander who has sacrificed her lifestyle to become a caretaker for our parents.

My Niece Stephanie R. Harris who has served as a nurse in the family.

To my Mother-in-Law Hester Lang and all of her children and grandchildren.

A special tribute to my sister-in-law Dorothy Lang who has sacrificed her lifestyle to become her mother's caretaker.

Special thanks to Eric and Shunika Stallworth for their love and support in my life.

To my Mt. Moriah Church Family, Faith Alive Christian Center Church Family, and my Columbus O'Banner Ministries partners and to all of my relatives, friends, and supporters.

Special Tribute to Columbus O'Banner Ministries Publication Administrator Anita Berry

TABLE OF CONTENTS

INTRODUCTION

*And all things, whatsoever ye shall ask in
prayer, believing, ye shall receive.*
Matthew 21:22

T he Lord spoke to my spirit in 2013 and He said to me that
Believers are Receivers. I started to think about what The
Lord had spoken to my spirit. Well if believers are receivers, then doubters do without. The Word of God only will work in the life of those who believe what God has spoken in His Word and has revealed in their spirit. So I came to the understanding; there are many people in the body of Christ that are not receiving what God has already provided for them in the finished work of Christ.

Jesus came to the earth from Heaven to destroy the works of the devil. Jesus came so that we could have life, a good life, where we would receive God's best in the earth and to spend eternity with God for ever. There are many people in the earth that are blinded to receiving their spirituals blessing from above.

In this book you will learn how to trust God in every area of your life. Also you will learn how to believe and how to receive, according to the Word of God. I will discuss three types of people in this book to better understand how important it is to be a spiritual believer.

1. The natural person or the non-believer.
2. The carnal person or the immature believer.
3. The spiritual person or the mature spiritual believer.

Which type of person are you? A non-believer, carnal believer, or a spiritual believer? Which type of person do you desire or plan on being?

At the end of this book you should know what type of person you are. Also you can become the person that God has designed you to be if you are not there yet.

To believe is to expect or hope with confidence; to trust. To receive is to embrace, to take a thing offered, or to accept. Believers are receivers and receivers are believers! Lord I believe, thank you! Believers are Receivers.

CHAPTER ONE

WHATSOEVER YOU ASK IN PRAYER

And all things, whatsoever ye shall ask in
prayer, believing, ye shall receive.
Matthew 21:22

W hen we ask God for His help, it shows our dependence upon Him. When we go to the Word of God, and find out what His will is for our life. We can receive the manifestation of the promises, by simply believing His Word! We are instructed in the Word of God to trust in God with all of our heart, and not to rely upon our own understanding about a matter. Prayer is communicating with God the Father about the will of God for your life! When we ask God for assistance according to His will, He will help us and come to our rescue. We cannot ask God to help us to do things against His will. Let's look at this scripture very close in:

Matthew 21:22
And all things, whatsoever ye shall ask in prayer, believing, ye shall receive.

"And all things," some people may think that no matter what they ask God, according to this scripture verse, they will receive. The key to this bible scripture is knowing what God has already provided for you in His Word. Let's look at another bible verse that will enlighten us on this particular matter.

2 Corinthians 1:20

[20] For all the promises of God in him are yea, and in him Amen, unto the glory of God by us.

Here we see that God only will bring to pass into your life what He has promised in Himself. So everything that He has promised in Him has been made available for you to receive as a believer in Christ. God our Heavenly Father will never provide us with anything outside of His will for our life. He will only provide us with all things that pertain to life and godliness. He is a good Father and He can only provide you with good things that are within His Nature. God is loving and kind, and He is good to all of His children. God has promised us life and life beyond measure.

When a believer read the bible, and truly believes In God, and the promises of God in His Word, the reality of these promises, start to manifest in his or her life. Believers are truly receivers, the only time people don't receive from The Lord is when they don't believe, or that they don't know His Word. The bible also say's can two walk together except they agree. You must be in agreement with the will of God to see the all things come to pass into your life, according to His Word.

So now let's look at "whatsoever ye ask in prayer." Whatsoever you ask God in communication; sometimes we don't know what to ask about a particular thing. That being the case, we can't ask with confidence. Therefore, the answer will not come into our life, if faith is not present. Without Faith in God, we cannot please Him. Faith begins were the will of God is known according to His Word. Once we know the will of God for our life and things that pertain to our life. We can approach Father God and ask for all the things that He has made available for us by His grace though Faith.

We should never pray for things that are not in the will of God for our lives. If we pray for things foolishly we will be disappointed, because God cannot answer a prayer that does not line up with His divine purpose and will. I have heard some people say sometimes God says yes and sometimes God says no. The only time you don't get a yes, is when you are not praying in line with the Word of God! The bible tells us that God watches over His Word to bring it to pass. You cannot believe God for something outside of His will for your life.

God is watching over His written Word! We are to put God in remembrance of His Covenant that He has provided for us Between Him and Jesus. The word of God says that we are heirs of God and joint heirs with Jesus Christ. God the Father, and God the Son, hath already made total provision for His Children in every area of their lives. Those that believe God, they receive from God. Believers are receivers, and doubters do without. Learn to say what is already written in the Word of God. The Word of God is forever settled. God has not changed in His way of doing things, He watches over His Word, so that it comes to pass in your life. Believers are Receivers.

Jeremiah 1:12
[12} Then said the Lord unto me, Thou hast well seen: for I will hasten my word to perform it.

CHAPTER TWO

ALL THINGS ARE POSSIBLE FOR THOSE WHO BELIEVE GOD

*Jesus said unto him, If thou canst believe, all things
are possible to him that believeth.*
Mark 9:23

I sn't that amazing that Jesus said that all things are possible to
Him that believeth. Sounds to me like, the problem lies in the
man believing the Word of God. If a man can believe right,
nothing is impossible for him to obtain. So we need to focus on the
things that can hinder us in believing God and His Word. One of the
things that can hinder our believing is unbelief. Unbelief will tell you
that the Word of God won't work for you. Unbelief will make you
feel like you are not worthy to receive a blessing from God.

Let's look into the Word of God and see the danger of unbelief in
the heart of a person or unbelief among a group of people.

Matthew 13:54-58
[54] And when he was come into his own country, he
taught them in their synagogue, insomuch that they were
astonished, and said, Whence hath this man this wisdom,
and these mighty works? [55] Is not this the carpenter's
son? is not his mother called Mary? and his brethren,
James, and Joses, and Simon, and Judas? [56] And his sisters, are they not all with us? Whence then hath this man
all these things? [57] And they were offended in him. But
Jesus said unto them, A prophet is not without honour,
save in his own country, and in his own house. [58] And

| 7

he did not many mighty works there because of their unbelief.

Here Jesus is sharing the Word of God with people from His
community, in which He was raised. They begin to discredit Him and
what He was teaching, because they knew Him, and His family members. Their hearts were filled with unbelief; and they became hard-
ened against the truth.

So we can see that unbelief is hearing and knowing the truth, but
not receiving the truth based upon your own reasoning or opinion.
Unbelief does not change the Word; it just won't allow the Word to
work for you, because belief and unbelief cannot be present in your
heart at the same time. If these people would have believed what Jesus shared with them, they would have received whatever they were
in need of from God the Father.

Today we see people in the earth who discredit godly leaders,
who hear from God. These men share amazing truth and the people
are astonished in the same way as when Jesus shared. Again pride
rises in their hearts, and they won't receive from God. They discredit
the power of the Word and the vessel that God has chosen to be a
mouth piece in the earth for Him. We saw it in the earth with Jesus,
and we see the same thing in the earth today.

The scripture also lets us know that the people were offended at
Jesus because, of the Wisdom of God and the mighty works of God;
that He shared with them. That lets us know that it is hard for some
people to receive the Word of God from certain individuals. Whenever this happens to someone who is sharing the Word of God; they
should just realize that those who are listening are operating in unbelief. If they did it do Jesus, you are not above Jesus; they will do it to
you. Just realize that you are in good company when you are accepted
or rejected; this happened in the life and ministry of Jesus.

Let's look at another danger that will keep us from believing God.
Tradition, yes tradition is very dangerous. Tradition will make the
powerful Word of God ineffective in your life; even though the Word
of God is never void of power. God's Word is powerful for believers,
because believers believe the Word of God. A tradition is something
that will draw or take your belief off of the Word of God. Traditions
can be your own rules and regulations in addition to the truth of The

Word of God. Anything that draws your attention away from the Word of God is a tradition of men, and present danger in you receiving the blessings of God though believing.

Matthew 15:1-9

[1] Then came to Jesus scribes and Pharisees, which were of Jerusalem, saying, [2] Why do thy disciples transgress the tradition of the elders? for they wash not their hands when they eat bread. [3] But he answered and said unto them, Why do ye also transgress the commandment of God by your tradition? [4] For God commanded, saying, Honour thy father and mother: and, He that curseth father or mother, let him die the death. [5] But ye say, Whosoever shall say to his father or his mother, It is a gift, by whatsoever thou mightest be profited by me; [6] And honour not his father or his mother, he shall be free . Thus have ye made the commandment of God of none effect by your tradition. [7] Ye hypocrites, well did Esaias prophesy of you, saying, [8] This people draweth nigh unto me with their mouth, and honoureth me with their lips; but their heart is far from me. [9] But in vain they do worship me, teaching for doctrines the commandments of men.

As you can see traditions; are doctrines of men, which go against the commandments of God. As you can see, it is very important to keep unbelief and the doctrines of men out of our hearts. Let's keep unbelief and tradition out of our hearts and believe God for the impossible. Believers are Receivers.

CHAPTER THREE

DON'T FORGET ABOUT YOUR BENEFIT PACKAGE IN GOD

Blessed be the Lord, who daily loadeth us with benefits,
even the God of our salvation. Selah.
Psalm 68:19

Praise The Lord for His goodness. A "Daily Benefit Plan", that God has provided for His Children. Everyday God is providing total protection and provision for His children. The only thing that's keeping His children from receiving their daily benefit is not believing, the truth of His Word. God is unloading daily blessings upon His children. But so many of His children won't receive what Jesus has made available in His life, death, burial, resurrection, and ascension, and His present position in Heaven right now as our Intercessor and High Priest. Jesus has provided us with everlasting life, divine health, divine wealth, long life, good days, peace and joy in the earth. He has given us authority and dominion in the earth.

Let's look at a job illustration. Some jobs have great benefit packages. Some jobs have employee benefit plans which may offer major medical, dental, and vision. However, if you as an employee are in need of some of the benefits within that package, even though it belongs to you as a employee, it does you no good if you are not knowledgeable about the benefits in order to receive the assistance. So it is in the natural, so it is in the spiritual.

There are a lot of people who work on jobs and don't know their rights, or benefits. Many people don't know about their benefits, unless someone takes the time to share those benefits with them. Employees should get a copy of their benefits to read and know them before or when they may need assistance.

Many of God's children are suffering in the earth, because they don't know what their benefits are as a child of God. All of God's benefits are written down in His will. We need to read, mediate, and study the will of God in His Word for our own life. Don't just wait for someone to share the benefits of God with you. They may not share the whole plan with you! Take the time to find out what God has provided for you in the whole plan of salvation. As a child of God, you are a part of the royal family of God. You have rights and privileges. You have become an heir of God and a joint-heir with Jesus. As many as received Jesus, became sons of God. Let's look at some of the benefits in:

Psalm 23:1-6
[1] The Lord is my shepherd; I shall not want. [2] He maketh me to lie down in green pastures: he leadeth me beside the still waters. [3] He restoreth my soul: he leadeth me in the paths of righteousness for his name's sake. [4] Yea, though I walk through the valley of the shadow of death, I will fear no evil: for thou art with me; thy rod and thy staff they comfort me. [5] Thou preparest a table before me in the presence of mine enemies: thou anointest my head with oil; my cup runneth over. [6] Surely goodness and mercy shall follow me all the days of my life: and I will dwell in the house of the Lord forever.

Here are some of your spiritual benefits

- The Lord is your Shepherd; He is your Provider and Protector.
- The Lord provides for you a green pasture, or a good life.
- The Lord leads you beside the still waters, or He orders your steps in His word.
- The Lord renews your mind within your soul and keeps you going in the right direction.

- The Lord is with you at all times, even when you are confronted with evil or trouble.
- The Lord makes total provision for you in the presence of those who hate or dislike you.
- The Lord causes you to live a life that is full of joy and manifested blessings in abundance.
- The Lord only will bring good things into your life. His goodness and mercy will rest upon your life.
- The Lord will keep you in His house where there are blessings for evermore.

Thank the Lord for His great spiritual benefits.
Believers are Receivers.

CHAPTER FOUR

BELIEVERS THINK UPON THE WORD OF GOD

This book of the law shall not depart out of thy mouth; but thou shalt meditate therein day and night, that thou mayest observe to do according to all that is written therein: for then thou shalt make thy way prosperous, and then thou shalt have good success.
Joshua 1:8

T o believe right, you have to think right; if you believe and think right; you will live right. If you believe right, you will do what is right.

You will have to keep the Word of God in your mouth, in order to do that. The Word of God must be in your heart. Whatever you think on or mediate upon will have the greater effect or influence upon your belief system. Thinking upon the Word of God, will uproot and remove erroneous thinking and wrong believing. If you believe wrong you will live wrong. If you think wrong, you will live wrong. As a person thinks, so is the life of that person lived out. If you will change the way you think, you will change the way you live.

It's insane to want a different outcome or result in your lifestyle without thinking and doing things differently. When people have a negative outlook in life, it's because their belief system has become negative and filled with doubtfulness or unbelief. Your mind is a very powerful tool; don't let it go to waste. Don't allow other people to use your mind, for their trash disposal. God made you too valuable to become the garbage pit for negativity. God instructs His children to keep their mind stayed upon Him. When you follow those instructions, and trust God, the peace of God will invade your heart and mind. The peace of God will effect and change your belief system. When the peace of God comes into your heart and mind, your outlook on life becomes positive. Then it becomes easy to receive from God, because it's easy to believe and see what the Father God has in store for you.

Believers are receivers, and doubters do without. God is a good God, and He loves His children. His desire is to bless His children beyond their desires, dreams, and imagination.

God is not withholding any good thing from His children. He only has good things and gifts for His children. The only requirement is to believe Him, and to receive from Him. Every good gift comes from above from the Father of light. God does not show partiality toward His children. In order, to receive from God as a believer; you must choose to keep your mind, focus and attention upon Him and His word.

Isaiah 26:3-4

[3] Thou wilt keep him in perfect peace, whose mind is stayed on thee : because he trusteth in thee. [4] Trust ye in the Lord for ever: for in the Lord Jehovah is everlasting strength:

In these verses of scripture, it is very clear, that we cannot allow bad things, circumstances, misunderstandings, distractions, trials, or tribulations to change our mindset about the everlasting strength of the Lord Jehovah, our provider in every area of our life. Being in perfect peace is the key to your provision. The Apostle Paul really shared some things in the New Testament on how to stay in perfect peace. Look at these portions of scriptures in:

Philippians 4:4-9

[4] Rejoice in the Lord alway: and again I say, Rejoice. [5] Let your moderation be known unto all men. The Lord is at hand. [6] Be careful for nothing; but in everything by prayer and supplication with thanksgiving let your requests be made known unto God. [7] And the peace of God, which passeth all understanding, shall keep your hearts and

minds through Christ Jesus. [8] Finally, brethren, whatsoever things are true, whatsoever things are honest, whatsoever things are just, whatsoever things are pure, whatsoever things are lovely, whatsoever things are of good report; if there be any virtue, and if there be any praise, think on these things. [9] Those things, which ye have both learned, and received, and heard, and seen in me, do: and the God of peace shall be with you.

To have perfected peace we must think on these things

- Whatsoever things are true.
- Whatsoever things are honest.
- Whatsoever things are just.
- Whatsoever things are pure.
- Whatsoever things are lovely.
- Whatsoever things are of a good report.
- Whatsoever things have virtue and that are worthy of praise.

If we allow the opposite of these things to be on our mind, or if we don't make a choice to mediate upon these, the peace of God will not abide within our lives. When the peace of God is missing in your life; your ability to believe God and His word becomes difficult. This is when doubt creeps in and blocks the blessings from God from being revealed in your life. Although everything has been provided for you in the finished works of Christ; it still requires faith in God to receive it.

This is the reason that the enemy of your faith; the devil is constantly making attempts to steal the Word of God out of your heart. The devil will do everything within his deceptive powers to keep you from spending time with God in prayer, studying the Word of God, or going to the church where God has placed you. Church a place where you are to hear the Word of God. The devil knows that if he can keep you from believing and receiving the truth of the Word of God that you will be deceived. He wants to get you out of faith and to get you operating in fear. Look at what the apostle James revealed in:

James 1:22-25

[22] But be ye doers of the word, and not hearers only, deceiving your own selves. [23] For if any be a hearer of the word, and not a doer, he is like unto a man beholding his natural face in a glass: [24] For he beholdeth himself, and goeth his way, and straightway forgetteth what manner of man he was. [25] But whoso looketh into the perfect law of liberty, and continueth therein , he being not a forgetful hearer, but a doer of the work, this man shall be blessed in his deed. Believers are Receivers.

CHAPTER FIVE

TRUSTING GOD

Trust in the Lord with all thine heart; and lean not unto thine own understanding.
Proverbs 3:5

Those that trust God will receive from God. To trust in God, is to depend upon His faithfulness to you. There may be things going on in your life that you may not understand. During these times it is very important to pray and allow the Word of God to be final authority in your life. During this time don't give up and don't allow doubt to keep you away from the blessings of God for you. When you trust God, you are demonstrating your confidence and faith in God. Once you settle in your heart, to do things God's way; you will always enjoy His blessings upon your life. Once you choose to honor God, and the way God does things; you will enjoy the good life. Let's look at some of these blessings in:

Proverbs 3:1-10
[1] My son, forget not my law; but let thine heart keep my commandments: [2] For length of days, and long life, and peace, shall they add to thee. [3] Let not mercy and truth forsake thee: bind them about thy neck; write them upon the table of thine heart: [4] So shalt thou find favour and good understanding in the sight of God and man. [5] Trust in the Lord with all thine heart; and lean not unto thine own understanding. [6] In all thy ways acknowledge him, and he shall direct thy paths. [7] Be not wise in thine own eyes: fear the Lord , and depart from evil. [8] It shall be

health to thy navel, and marrow to thy bones. [9] Honour the Lord with thy substance, and with the firstfruits of all thine increase: [10] So shall thy barns be filled with plenty, and thy presses shall burst out with new wine.

Here are some of the additional Benefits
in Trusting God

- ◆ God will place honor upon those who honor Him.
- ◆ God will increase the number of your days upon the earth.
- ◆ God will bless you to live a long life upon the earth.
- ◆ God will cause you to live in peace, when you face storms in your life, the peace of God will sustain you.
- ◆ Trusting God will keep the peace of God in your life which; will cause you to live a life, free from stress.
- ◆ Trusting God will cause you to operate in the favor of God upon your life.
- ◆ Trusting God will cause you to have the favor of God with people that you come into contact with for kingdom business.
- ◆ In trusting God you will have a good understanding with God and about your relationship with God.
- ◆ When you trust God your understanding of things will be good among people.
- ◆ When you trust God, you can live a healthy and wealthy lifestyle.

When you truly trust in God, you will walk in the blessing of the Lord. Some people may say with their mouth, that they trust God; but in their heart, they really don't trust God. A parrot can learn how to repeat words after you, but that parrot doesn't believe you. That parrot is simply repeating your words.

Saying the right things in life is good, but believing the right things is more important. You see, you can say the right things in life, but if you don't believe what you say, those things won't become a reality in your life. I am sure that your eyes have been open with this simple illustration. Those that really believe the words in their heart, before or when they speak them will, receive what they believe. The works of God are to believe God. When you believe God, you have entered into the rest of God.

John 14:10-14

[10] Believest thou not that I am in the Father, and the Father in me? the words that I speak unto you I speak not of myself: but the Father that dwelleth in me, he doeth the works. [11] Believe me that I am in the Father, and the Father in me: or else believe me for the very works' sake. [12] Verily, verily, I say unto you, He that believeth on me, the works that I do shall he do also; and greater works than these shall he do; because I go unto my Father. [13] And whatsoever ye shall ask in my name, that will I do, that the Father may be glorified in the Son. [14] If ye shall ask any thing in my name, I will do it.

Anything that you can believe God for according to His will, you can receive from God. Just asks. Believers are Receivers.

CHAPTER SIX

THERE ARE THREE TYPES OF PEOPLE IN THE WORLD

But the natural man receiveth not the things of the Spirit of God:
for they are foolishness unto him: neither can he know them ,
because they are spiritually discerned.
1 Corinthians 2:14

I n this chapter, I will like to talk about the three types of people in the world. I would like to talk about the natural man, the carnal man and the spiritual man.

The natural man is a person who does not have a person relationship with the Lord Jesus Christ. This person is also known as a sinner, or an unbeliever in the world. The man that is not born-again, is physically alive, but spiritually dead, or separated from God. The natural man may know about God, but he does not know God in a personal relationship. The natural man is the man, who has not received Jesus as his Lord and Savior.

On the other hand there are two types of believers or christians upon the earth. There are carnal christians, and spiritual christians. Let's take a look at the carnal christians first.

The carnal christian is a born-again christian, which still thinks and lives like the non-believer in a number of ways. A carnal christian is a believer who had decided to walk in a mindset that opposes God.

On the other hand, the spiritual christian is a believer that is spiritually mature, being led by the Spirit of God. This type of believer chooses to be led by the Spirit of God, living by faith in God, and having the mindset of Christ. This believer is trusting in the grace of

God, and the finished works of Christ. Let's take a look at these scripture in:

1 Corinthians 2:9-14

[9] But as it is written, Eye hath not seen, nor ear heard, neither have entered into the heart of man, the things which God hath prepared for them that love him. [10] But God hath revealed them unto us by his Spirit: for the Spirit searcheth all things, yea, the deep things of God. [11] For what man knoweth the things of a man, save the spirit of man which is in him? even so the things of God knoweth no man, but the Spirit of God. [12] Now we have received, not the spirit of the world, but the spirit which is of God; that we might know the things that are freely given to us of God. [13] Which things also we speak, not in the words which man's wisdom teacheth, but which the Holy Ghost teacheth; comparing spiritual things with spiritual. [14] But the natural man receiveth not the things of the Spirit of God: for they are foolishness unto him: neither can he know them , because they are spiritually discerned.

We can conclude according to the scripture, that the things of God, don't make sense to a man that is not spiritual. It is very important to be a spiritually mature believer. God is a good Father and He will only give to you what you are able to properly handle in this life. How much you receive from God is based on how much you can believe Him for in faith, according to what Christ has already provided for you, before the foundation of the world. Believers are Receivers.

CHAPTER SEVEN

BELIEVE THAT YOU RECEIVE IN PRAYER

Therefore I say unto you, What things soever ye desire,
when ye pray, believe that ye receive them ,
and ye shall have them.
Mark 11:24

What does it mean to believe that you receive in prayer? You must believe in your heart in faith before you pray, that God has already granted your desire in prayer. You must believe the answer to your prayer before you ask God in prayer. To have this kind of faith, you must pray according to the will of God, and the Word of God. Faith begins where the will of God is known.

Every answer to prayer is already in the finished works of Christ; all of the promises of God are yes and amen. Those that believe God in prayer, make the greatness of His mighty power available in their life. Prayer will allow the power of God to get involved in your life to give you the assistance that you need to win in life.

Jesus also said that those who pray in secret, God will reward them openly. Let's look at a prayer that the Apostle Paul prayed in:

Ephesians 1:16-23

[16] Cease not to give thanks for you, making mention of you in my prayers; [17] That the God of our Lord Jesus Christ, the Father of glory, may give unto you the spirit of wisdom and revelation in the knowledge of him: [18] The eyes of your understanding being enlightened; that ye may know what is the hope of his calling, and what the riches of the glory of his inheritance in the saints, [19] And what is the exceeding greatness of his power to us-ward who believe, according to the working of his mighty power, [20] Which he wrought in Christ, when he raised him from the dead, and set him at his own right hand in the heavenly places , [21] Far above all principality, and power, and might, and dominion, and every name that is named, not only in this world, but also in that which is to come: [22] And hath put all things under his feet, and gave him to be the head over all things to the church, [23] Which is his body, the fulness of him that filleth all in all.

As you can see, the only problem that believers have in life, is when they don't know their rights in Christ. The Apostle Paul's prayer was that the believers spiritual eyes would be open to the finished works of Christ. I believe, that we should pray that our brothers and sisters in Christ spiritual eyes would be open to these truths:

- ◆ That the Father of Glory, give unto them the spirit of wisdom and the revelation in the knowledge of Him.
- ◆ That the eyes of their understanding being open, to know what is the hope of their calling, and what belongs to them though inheritance as believers in Christ.
- ◆ That believers should know what has been made available to them though the resurrection of Christ and His position at the right hand of the Father.

Let's look at another prayer that the Apostle Paul prayed in:

Ephesians 3:14-21 KJV

[14] For this cause I bow my knees unto the Father of our Lord Jesus Christ, [15] Of whom the whole family in heaven and earth is named, [16] That he would grant you, according to the riches of his glory, to be strengthened with might by his Spirit in the inner man; [17] That Christ may dwell in their hearts by faith; that ye, being rooted and grounded in love, [18] May be able to comprehend with all saints what is the breadth, and length, and depth, and height; [19] And to know the love of Christ, which passeth knowledge, that ye might be filled with all the fulness of God. [20] Now unto him that is able to do exceeding abundantly above all that we ask or think, according to the power that worketh in us, [21] Unto him be glory in the church by Christ Jesus throughout all ages, world without end. Amen.

Here we see the Apostle Paul in prayer to our Heavenly Father. He prayed and asked the Father to grant his request:

♦ That the Father would grant the believers according to the riches of His glory, to be strengthen with might by His Spirit in the inner man.
♦ That Christ may dwell in the believer's hearts by faith.
♦ That the believers be rooted and grounded in love.
♦ That the believers would be able to comprehend, with all the saints, so they would not be behind in their spiritual understanding.
♦ That the believers would know how much God loves them, which exceeds their knowledge, and that the believers would operate in the fullness of God.

According to the Word of God; God is able to do exceedingly beyond what we can ask or think according to His power that dwells in us. Also we see that the power is on the inside of us dwelling in the inner man or the spiritual man. This is the real you, this is the person who is made in the image of God, and His likeness.

To pray for other believers is very important. It demonstrates to God, that you are loving, and caring about other people, and not just thinking about yourself and your needs being met. Also you are being obedient to His will for your life.

I don't believe that the body of Christ as a whole understands how important it is to have a strong and a consistent prayer life, and foundation. Some people make so many decisions in life, without talking to God our Father about it. The Word of God, instructs us to acknowledge God in all of our ways. Every decision that we make, should be made after we talk to God about it, and wait upon His answer. God is interested in every area of our life. We should talk to Him about major and minor decisions. Prayer is communicating with God. When a believer talks to their Heavenly Father, they should be sincere and honest. They should pray according to the Word. God's Word is true, just put God in remembrance of His Word or repeat His Word back to Him, or what He has promised in His Word to you. We are to pray without ceasing, according to the Word; we are to give thanks in all things. We should thanks God for His grace, His goodness, His faithfulness, His mercy, His love, His protection, and His provision. Believers are Receivers.

CHAPTER EIGHT

BELIEVERS ENTERING INTO THE REST OF GOD

Let us labour therefore to enter into that rest, lest any man
fall after the same example of unbelief.
Hebrews 4:11

As believers, we are to trust in what God has already provided for us though faith. Our labor is to rest and have confidence in what God has already done in Christ. In the finished works of Christ everything has already being accomplished for the believer.

Our salvation is a free gift from God the Father though faith. We are saved by Grace though Faith; there is only one way to receive salvation. Jesus said that He was the only way to come into a relationship with the Father. Jesus came that we would have the life of God, and a blessed life in the earth. This plan was in the heart and mind of God before the foundation of the world. This is the gospel or good news concerning the love of the Father. The only requirement is to believe what God has already spoken and already done.

We must enter into the finished works of Christ, and not trust in our own work, or self efforts. To rest in the Lord is to cease from our own way of doing things. Once we believe the gospel of grace, or the finished works of Christ, we enter into the rest of God, and cease from our own labor. The only labor that we have been called to do is to trust God and to have faith.

In His Word, when you believe God, you will be in a position to receive from God. Without faith it is impossible to please God. You must believe that God is the true God, and that He will reward those who seek after Him. Whenever a person does not believe God, they fall into unbelief. To enter into unbelief is to have a heart that is hard toward God, and the things that pertain to The Kingdom of God. The Kingdom of God is God's righteousness, God's Peace, and joy in the Holy Spirit. Whenever a person chooses to reject the Kingdom of God, they are putting their belief in a system or a way of doing things that is inspired by the enemy of God; the devil. It is very important to trust God as your source. We should not put anything before God. He should be first within our life. Look in:

Hebrews 4:1-11

[1] Let us therefore fear, lest, a promise being left us of entering into his rest, any of you should seem to come short of it. [2] For unto us was the gospel preached, as well as unto them: but the word preached did not profit them, not being mixed with faith in them that heard it . [3] For we which have believed do enter into rest, as he said, As I have sworn in my wrath, if they shall enter into my rest: although the works were finished from the foundation of the world. [4] For he spake in a certain place of the seventh day on this wise, And God did rest the seventh day from all his works. [5] And in this place again, If they shall enter into my rest. [6] Seeing therefore it remaineth that some must enter therein, and they to whom it was first preached entered not in because of unbelief: [7] Again, he limiteth a certain day, saying in David, To day, after so long a time; as it is said, Today if ye will hear his voice, harden not your hearts. [8] For if Jesus had given them rest, then would he not afterward have spoken of another day. [9] There remaineth therefore a rest to the people of God. [10] For he that is entered into his rest, he also hath ceased from his own works, as God did from his. [11] Let us labour therefore to enter into that rest, lest any man fall after the same example of unbelief.

Thank God for giving us so many great examples to learn from in His Holy Word. Would you declare this with me today?

"I have entered into the rest of God. I have creased from my own works, and now I am resting in the finished works of Christ. Thank you Father for your grace and your mercy, Jesus you have already provided everything that I will ever need. Amen."

Believers are Receivers.

CHAPTER NINE

BELIEVERS SHARING THE GOSPEL OF CHRIST

And he said unto them, Go ye into all the world, and
preach the gospel to every creature.
Mark 16:15

B elievers have been commissioned by Jesus to share the gospel into all the world to every person. Those that believe this gospel will receive salvation. Those that reject this gospel that is preached will continue to walk in condemnation; and to remain disconnected from God our Heavenly Father. Those that believe in the preaching of the Word of God will walk in spiritual authority in the earth.

The Lord works with those who believe the preaching of the gospel of the kingdom, which is the gospel of grace. This is a great assignment given unto believers in the family of God. We have been given the privilege and the right to share God's plan of salvation to those who are sinners. What an honor to be able to share the gospel of our Lord and Savior Jesus Christ. Once we become obedient to the great commission, the blessing of The Lord is resting upon our life. Also, Jesus our Lord is confirming the word that we preach with signs and wonders. Praise The Lord! Believers have the Word of God being confirmed by The Lord! Look in the following scriptures:

Mark 16:15-20
[15] And he said unto them, Go ye into all the world, and preach the gospel to every creature. [16] He that believeth and is baptized shall be saved; but he that believeth not

shall be damned. [17] And these signs shall follow them that believe; In my name shall they cast out devils; they shall speak with new tongues; [18] They shall take up serpents; and if they drink any deadly thing, it shall not hurt them; they shall lay hands on the sick, and they shall recover. [19] So then after the Lord had spoken unto them, he was received up into heaven, and sat on the right hand of God. [20] And they went forth, and preached everywhere, the Lord working with them , and confirming the word with signs following. Amen.

The Bible tells us that God is not willing, for any person to depart from this earth without receiving Jesus as their Lord and Savior. We as believers are the only people in the earth that God has chosen to live in and to work in and to work though upon the earth.

When the first man that God created named Adam sinned against God, all men born into the world were born sinners though natural birth; with the exception of Jesus Christ. Jesus birth was very special and without sin. Jesus was God wrapped up in a physical body and He came down from heaven into the earth. With this being the case, you can see that man being born apart from God is a sinner. The only way for a person to be saved, is to become a believer! Believers are Receivers of God's plan of salvation. As many as receive Jesus they become sons of God. Let's take a look at a very well known set of scriptures in:

John 3:16-18

[16] For God so loved the world, that he gave his only begotten Son, that whosoever believeth in him should not perish, but have everlasting life. [17] For God sent not his Son into the world to condemn the world; but that the world through him might be saved. [18] He that believeth on him is not condemned: but he that believeth not is condemned already, because he hath not believed in the name of the only begotten Son of God.

Thank God for Jesus. Believers are Receivers.

CHAPTER TEN

"BELIEVE ONLY"

But when Jesus heard it , he answered him, saying, Fear not:
believe only, and she shall be made whole.
Luke 8:50

To believe God only is to bring the power of God into operation within your life, and the life of others. To believe only is to believe God above the natural condition that exists in your life, or the condition or someone else's life. Your spirit was created to believe God, no matter what obstacles you are confronted with.

To believe only, is to believe with your spirit or to believe with your heart. God is a Spirit, and you must believe God with your spirit. When you believe God with your spirit all things become possible in your life.

In Jesus earthly ministry He healed a lot of people, and He did many miracles, for those who would only believe Him. To believe only, is to believe beyond, the five physical senses, your sight, hearing, taste, touch, or feeling. The Apostle Paul stated that we walk by Faith and not by sight. In other words, we walk by what we believe and not by what we see or perceive according to the five physical senses. God gave us physical senses to operate in the physical world, and He gave us faith to operate in the spiritual world. Once you believe God or have faith in God, you are granted access to spiritual or heavenly blessings in your life, and in the life of others.

To believe only, is being able to believe the Word of God above what you can see, hear, feel, taste, or touch in your physical life. Once a person can believe only, they can know, and experience what

God has made available for them according to His Word in the finished works of Christ.

To believe only, is not to allow doubt to come into your spirit or spiritual heart. Your spirit is made in the image and likeness of God, and your spirit was created to believe only God. Your spirit agrees with God and allows you to walk with God. Your spirit is what the Apostle Paul, referred to as the inner man. The inner man is the person who will never die, or who will live with God throughout eternity. Let's look at some cases in the Word of God, where to believe only caused the miraculous to take place:

Luke 8:41-56

[41] And, behold, there came a man named Jairus, and he was a ruler of the synagogue: and he fell down at Jesus' feet, and besought him that he would come into his house: [42] For he had one only daughter, about twelve years of age, and she lay a dying. But as he went the people thronged him. [43] And a woman having an issue of blood twelve years, which had spent all her living upon physicians, neither could be healed of any, [44] Came behind him , and touched the border of his garment: and immediately her issue of blood stanched. [45] And Jesus said, Who touched me? When all denied, Peter and they that were with him said, Master, the multitude throng thee and press thee , and sayest thou, Who touched me? [46] And Jesus said, Somebody hath touched me: for I perceive that virtue is gone out of me. [47] And when the woman saw that she was not hid, she came trembling, and falling down before him, she declared unto him before all the people for what cause she had touched him, and how she was healed immediately. [48] And he said unto her, Daughter, be of good comfort: thy faith hath made thee whole; go in peace. [49] While he yet spake, there cometh one from the ruler of the synagogue's house , saying to him, Thy daughter is dead; trouble not the Master. [50] But when Jesus heard it , he answered him, saying, Fear not: believe only, and she shall be made whole. [51] And when he came into the

house, he suffered no man to go in, save Peter, and James, and John, and the father and the mother of the maiden. [52] And all wept, and bewailed her: but he said, Weep not; she is not dead, but sleepeth. [53] And they laughed him to scorn, knowing that she was dead. [54] And he put them all out, and took her by the hand, and called, saying, Maid, arise. [55] And her spirit came again, and she arose straightway: and he commanded to give her meat. [56] And her parents were astonished: but he charged them that they should tell no man what was done.

We are told in the Word of God, that Jesus did so many miracles, that there is not a book large enough to contain all the miracles He did upon the earth. To believe only, is to say I trust only in you Lord. You can have doubt in your mind, and still believe only in your spirit and still be pleasing to God. Let's look at a man who has unbelief in his mind, but believed in his heart that Jesus could help his son:

Mark 9:17-29
[17] And one of the multitude answered and said, Master, I have brought unto thee my son, which hath a dumb spirit; [18] And wheresoever he taketh him, he teareth him: and he foameth, and gnasheth with his teeth, and pineth away: and I spake to thy disciples that they should cast him out; and they could not. [19] He answereth him, and saith, O faithless generation, how long shall I be with you? how long shall I suffer you? bring him unto me. [20] And they brought him unto him: and when he saw him, straightway the spirit tare him; and he fell on the ground, and wallowed foaming. [21] And he asked his father, How long is it ago since this came unto him? And he said, Of a child. [22] And ofttimes it hath cast him into the fire, and into the waters, to destroy him: but if thou canst do any thing, have compassion on us, and help us. [23] Jesus said unto him, If thou canst believe, all things are possible to him that believeth. [24] And straightway the father of the child cried out, and said with tears, Lord, I believe; help thou mine

unbelief. [25] When Jesus saw that the people came running together, he rebuked the foul spirit, saying unto him, Thou dumb and deaf spirit, I charge thee, come out of him, and enter no more into him. [26] And the spirit cried, and rent him sore, and came out of him: and he was as one dead; insomuch that many said, He is dead. [27] But Jesus took him by the hand, and lifted him up; and he arose. [28] And when he was come into the house, his disciples asked him privately, Why could not we cast him out? [29] And he said unto them, This kind can come forth by nothing, but by prayer and fasting.

Jesus knew exactly where the father's level of faith was for his son. In the natural when all hope is gone, the Word of God will work for you. If you only believe God against what appears to be no hope in the natural. Believe God, He will come through for you.

Jesus knew that the disciples were not operating in faith, when the father of the boy, brought him to them. We must be prayed up, which will cause our flesh to be disciplined, so when people come to us to get help we are prepared. Even though we pray and fast, we must still believe only in God, to see the blessings of God operating in or upon a person's life. The self righteous and religious people of the earth, during the time of Jesus earthy ministry would pray and fast often; but never received from God, because they did not believe in their heart.

Believe only, people of God, and get ready for your blessings, breakthroughs, miracles, or whatever it is that you need from God. To believe only, is to expect only to receive from God only. God will never fail you, or let you down, when you put or place your trust, confidence or belief in Him. To believe only is to do only what God tells or instructs you to do. When people would believe only in Jesus; blinded eyes were opened, paralyzed people took up their beds and walked, lepers were made clean and some made whole. Some People who had demons were made free. Still others, who believed only, saw their dead raised from the dead.

When Jesus saw people who needed a miracle from God, He did not ask them to pray for a season, nor did He ask them to fast for a season. Jesus asked people who needed a miracle or desired something from the Father God to believe only. Jesus always got people to use their faith in God in order to receive from God.

Faith in God is to believe what God has already done or said in His Word. Those who allow doubt to enter into their heart or spirit do without. All things are possible, if you only believe! Believers are Receivers.

CHAPTER ELEVEN

HOW TO PROTECT MY NEW HEART AS A BELIEVER

Keep thy heart with all diligence; for out of it
are the issues of life.
Proverbs 4:23

I t is very important to guard your new heart away from the things that can pollute your heart. Your new heart or spirit was made to believe God and His Word. Your new heart already is in agreement with God. Once you became born-again from death to life, the life of God started operating within your new heart.

Now you have to guard your heart on purpose from the old way of living, thinking and being. You cannot allow the things of the world that are corrupt to enter into your new heart. You now have to be consistent to attend to the Word of God. You must be selective in your hearing, seeing, and thinking. Everything that you need from God is already within your new spirit. We must not allow wrong words or negative words, filled with unbelief to enter into our physical or spiritual ears. We must monitor what we allow our physical and spiritual eyes to see or watch. So you must choose from within, being lead by the Holy Spirit on what you should embrace or reject within your heart. Every part of your being belongs to God. That includes your spirit, your soul, and your physical body. Your spirit has been made right with God, once you received Jesus as your Lord and Savior.

On the other hand, you must be intentional on purpose to renew your mind and to discipline your body to obey God. Your spirit has the power within to live a righteous and holy life that is pleasing to God. When you became born-again, God placed a part of Himself of

His Spirit within your spirit. Now your spirit is made to walk in authority and dominion in the earth once again. Now you are more than a conqueror in this earth. God and you are walking together now in the earth as one. You are now one Spirit with the Lord. Now you are like God within your new spirit. Now you can function like God in the Earth as a son of God, this is how Jesus functioned in the earth as the Son of God and the Son of Man.

The bible says that now we are the sons of God. God our Father is the Creator of all things by the words of His mouth. We also have been given this ability to create the things within our life by the words we speak or declare. This is the reason that it is so vital that we speak in line with the Word of God. Just agree and declare what God has already said. Don't allow the wrong things or words to enter into your believing heart and to speak, say, or to communicate the wrong things or words. Your words come to pass in your life, whether they are good words or idle words. Whatever you sow, you will reap the harvest. Whatever you speak will come to pass within your life. Whatever you plant within your life, you will grow to harvest. Whatever you believe you will receive. Take a close look at:

Proverbs 4:20-27

[20] My son, attend to my words; incline thine ear unto my sayings. [21] Let them not depart from thine eyes; keep them in the midst of thine heart. [22] For they are life unto those that find them, and health to all their flesh. [23] Keep thy heart with all diligence; for out of it are the issues of life. [24] Put away from thee a froward mouth, and perverse lips put far from thee. [25] Let thine eyes look right on, and let thine eyelids look straight before thee. [26] Ponder the path of thy feet, and let all thy ways be established. [27] Turn not to the right hand nor to the left: remove thy foot from evil. The bible say's that an unbelieving heart is considered to be an evil heart. What makes an unbelieving heart evil; because your heart was made to believe God. Look at what the Word has to say about that in Hebrews 3:12 KJV [12] Take heed, brethren, lest there be

in any of you an evil heart of unbelief, in departing from the living God.

An evil heart is a deceived heart that has departed from the life of God, and now believes the lies of the devil. You must put on the whole armor of God to stand against the schemes of the enemy. Believers guard your heart, so you can walk in the life that God your Father, has already provided for you in Christ Jesus. Believers are Receivers.

CHAPTER TWELVE

BELIEVERS ARE WORLD OVERCOMERS

Who is he that overcometh the world, but he that believeth that
Jesus is the Son of God?
1 John 5:5

P raise God for Jesus the Son of the living God. Those that believe that Jesus is the Son of God are world overcomers. The world has no power over the believer. Believers are receivers in every area of their life. To believe God, is to receive and to accept the Word of God, as final authority in your life. The Word of God is true, because in the beginning was the Word, and the Word was with God, and the Word was God. It is impossible for God to lie. God gave us His Word, to let us know how much that He loves us.

He is our Father, and He provides and protects His children from all hurt, harm, and danger. We can live a life of victory as children of God. We can walk in the authority of the believer, because God created us to have dominion in the earth. Darkness can never put out that light; because light will always shine in darkness, no matter how dark it is. To believe right, your focus on spiritual things must be consistent, based upon the truth of God's word. We must not try to figure out in our minds, how God is going to work things out in our life. Our responsibility is to trust and obey His Word. In doing so, we will receive that which we believe, according to His Word and His will for our lives. It is the will of God for His children to live and walk in victory each and everyday.

Before the fall of man in the Garden of Eden; Man never knew or experienced loneliness, depression, sickness, confusion, lack, strife, turmoil, or fear. Before the fall of man in the Garden of Eden; he lived and walked in the glory of God. He walked in his authority and operated in his dominion in the earth. He spent time in the presence of God everyday communicating with His Father and Creator. He believed everything that God told him, he never questioned or doubted God his Father. He was not afraid of God. Man never knew of storms such as hurricanes, tornados, or floods. Man never had or experienced a bad day or a struggle before his separation from God.

Even though we have opposition in the earth now from the devil, we can still live in victory and not be a victim of things in the earth that don't please God. Once we believe the Word of God in our hearts, we get the victory in Christ Jesus. The greater one lives in you, and you are victorious. This is your season for grace, favor, and greatness. Let this be your declaration. The greater has come into my life. Believers are Receivers.

BELIEVERS ARE RECEIVERS CONFESSION

I am a believer, therefore I am a receiver. I believe that a greater grace has come upon my life as a believer. I believe in the finished works of Christ, therefore I receive everything that Jesus has provided for me; in His death, burial, resurrection, and ascension. Greater grace has come upon my life and there is a greater anointing operating in and upon my life. This year I am operating in greater grace and favor. I am experiencing greater health in my mind and in my physical body. I am increasing with greater wealth and riches in my life. Jesus said that I would do the same works, and the greater works, because He is going unto the Father. Therefore there is a greater anointing upon my life, my calling, and my ministry. There is also a greater anointing upon my family and friends for break-throughs and victories in their life. Because I am a believer, I am a receiver, I trust in the finished works of Christ. Therefore I enter into His rest by faith, and cease from my own labor. Jesus has done it all for me, therefore I am a receiver, because I am a believer. Believers Are Receivers. Amen.

CONCLUSION

T hank you for taking the time to invest in this book, thank you for your prayers over my life, calling, and ministry. Thank you for sharing your thoughts with your friends about Believers are Receivers. Thank you for trusting God in your life and allowing His perfect will to be done in you! May you have and experience God's best in your life.

Your friend in Christ, Columbus O'Banner Jr.

Prayer Of Salvation

Romans 3:23
[23] For all have sinned, and come short of the glory of God;

John 3:16
[16] For God so loved the world, that he gave his only begotten Son, that whosoever believeth in him should not perish, but have everlasting life.

John 1:12
[12] But as many as received him, to them gave he power to become the sons of God, even to them that believe on his name:

Acts 2:21
[21] And it shall come to pass, that whosoever shall call on the name of the Lord shall be saved.

Romans 10:8-10
[8] But what saith it? The word is nigh thee, even in thy mouth, and in thy heart: that is, the word of faith, which we preach; [9] That if thou shalt confess with thy mouth the Lord Jesus, and shalt believe in thine heart that God hath raised him from the dead, thou shalt be saved. [10] For with the heart man believeth unto righteousness; and with the mouth confession is made unto salvation.

God loves you regardless of your life. God sent His own Son, Jesus to die on the cross for the sins of the human race. Jesus died and rose again for your justification. If you would like to receive Jesus into your life, please pray this prayer sincerely from your heart, confessing with your mouth:

> Heavenly Father, I come to you right now admitting to you that I am a sinner. I believe that Jesus died on the cross for my sins and that He rose again from the dead on the third day. Heavenly Father, I come to You in the Name of Jesus. Your Word says, "whosoever shall call on the name of the Lord shall be saved." I am calling on you. I pray and ask Jesus to come into my heart and be Lord over my life according to your Word found in:

Romans 10:9-10

> [9] That if thou shalt confess with thy mouth the Lord Jesus, and shalt believe in thine heart that God hath raised him from the dead, thou shalt be saved. [10] For with the heart man believeth unto righteousness; and with the mouth confession is made unto salvation. I do that right now.

> I confess that Jesus is Lord, and I believe in my heart that God raised Him from the dead. Thank you, Father, for saving me by your grace though faith in the name of Jesus Christ. Amen.

PRAYER TO RECEIVE THE BAPTISM IN THE HOLY SPIRIT

Luke 11:13
[13] If ye then, being evil, know how to give good gifts unto your children: how much more shall your heavenly Father give the Holy Spirit to them that ask him?

John 7:38
[38] He that believeth on me, as the scripture hath said, out of his belly shall flow rivers of living water.

Romans 8:26-27
[26] Likewise the Spirit also helpeth our infirmities: for we know not what we should pray for as we ought: but the Spirit itself maketh intercession for us with groanings which cannot be uttered. [27] And he that searcheth the hearts knoweth what is the mind of the Spirit, because he maketh intercession for the saints according to the will of God.

Acts 1:8
[8] But ye shall receive power, after that the Holy Ghost is come upon you: and ye shall be witnesses unto me both in Jerusalem, and in all Judaea, and in Samaria, and unto the uttermost part of the earth.

Acts 2:1-4
[1] And when the day of Pentecost was fully come, they were all with one accord in one place. [2] And suddenly

there came a sound from heaven as of a rushing mighty wind, and it filled all the house where they were sitting. [3] And there appeared unto them cloven tongues like as of fire, and it sat upon each of them. [4] And they were all filled with the Holy Ghost, and began to speak with other tongues, as the Spirit gave them utterance.

Jude 1:20

[20] But ye, beloved, building up yourselves on your most holy faith, praying in the Holy Ghost,

If you desire to be filled with the Holy Spirit since you are now the righteousness of God in Christ Jesus. Please pray this prayer in faith:

Father I have received Jesus as my Lord and Savior. I am a child of the Almighty God. I am born again. I am a Christian. I am a new creature in Christ Jesus. I am the righteousness of God in Christ Jesus. I am saved! Father now I am asking you to fill me with the Holy Spirit with the evidence of speaking in other tongues, as the Spirit of God gives me the utterance in Jesus Name. Amen. Father, I praise you and I thank you for filling me with the Holy Spirit. Amen

You are now a born-again, spirit-filled believer and we are glad that you are in the family of God and have become an effective witness in the body of Christ. Now, start out by reading the gospel of John, pray each day, and let the Spirit of The Lord lead you to the right church where the Word is being taught and there exists the spirit of liberty.

ABOUT THE AUTHOR

Now the just shall live by faith:
Hebrews 10:38a

Pastor Columbus O'Banner Jr. is a native of Jackson, Mississippi. He and his loving wife Barbara, currently reside in Byram, Mississippi. Together they have four children and seven grandchildren. They serve as Pastors at Mt. Moriah Church located in Magee, Mississippi, and Faith Alive Christian Center located in Byram, Mississippi.

Pastor Columbus O'Banner Jr. also is the founder and CEO of Columbus O'Banner Ministries and is the host of a weekly Christian broadcast, "Living by Faith," which airs on the PEG Comcast Cable Channel 18. "Living by Faith" is presently airing on Saturday evening at 10:30 pm in the Jackson Metro Area.

Pastor Columbus O'Banner Jr. gave his life to Christ on August 3, 1977. The following year he received the baptism in the Holy Spirit on February 2, 1978.

Pastor Columbus O'Banner Jr. and his wife are graduates of Word of Life Bible Training Center and ordained ministers of Word of Life Ministerial Association. They are also members of Creflo Dollar Ministerial Association (CDMA), founded by Dr. Creflo A Dollar and Fellowship of International Christian Word of Faith Ministries (FICWFM), founded by Apostle Dr. Frederick K.C. Price.

Pastor Columbus O'Banner Jr. published his first written book in December 2012. The title of that book is "Living The Good Life".

Pastors Columbus & Barbara O'Banner heart's desire is to see the body of Christ operating in love, faith, and unity. The bible says that there is One Lord, one Faith, one Baptism (Ephesians 4:5). God has called His people to operate in honor, excellence, and divine order. Their emphasis is based on teaching the uncompromising Word of God.

Columbus O'Banner Ministries
P .O. Box 824
Magee, MS 39111
cobanner@comcast.net

www.ingramcontent.com/pod-product-compliance
Lightning Source LLC
Chambersburg PA
CBHW070026110426
42741CB00034B/2640